DATE DUE

OCT 22 2009	
OCT 22 2009	
SEP 22 2016	

DEMCO, INC. 38-2931

THE SCIENCE OF

FORCES

PROJECTS AND EXPERIMENTS WITH FORCES AND MACHINES

© 2005 Heinemann Library
a division of Reed Elsevier Inc.
Chicago, Illinois

Customer Service 888-454-2279
Visit our website at www.heinemannlibrary.com

Designer: Gary Jeffrey
Editor: Gail Bushnell
Picture Research: Gail Bushnell

09 08 07 06 05
10 9 8 7 6 5 4 3 2 1

Library of Congress Cataloging-in-Publication Data

Parker, Steve.
    The science of forces : projects and experiments with forces and machines /
Steve Parker.
        p. cm.
    Includes bibliographical references and index.
    ISBN 1-4034-7285-8 (lib. bdg. : alk. paper) -- ISBN 1-4034-7292-0 (pbk. :
alk.paper)
    1. Force and energy--Experiments--Juvenile literature. 2. Power
(Mechanics)--Experiments--Juvenile literature. I. Title.
    QC73.4.P394 2005
    531'.6--dc22
                                        2005006947

Acknowledgments
The author and publisher are grateful to the following for permission to reproduce copyright material:
Pages 4t & m, 6tl & tr, 14tr, 18tl, 26tl, – Corbis Images. 14l – NASA. 8m, 12 (Sipa Press);
20mr (Nova Stock); 22tl (Bob Walls); 24tr – Rex Features Ltd.

With special thanks to the models: Meshach Burton, Sam Heming De-Allie, Annabel Garnham, Andrew Gregson, Hannah Holmes, Molly Rose Ibbett, Margaux Monfared, Max Monfared, Charlotte Moore, Beth Shon, Meg Shon, William Slater, Danielle Smale and Pippa Stannard.

Every effort has been made to contact copyright holders of any material reproduced in this book. Any omissions will be rectified in subsequent printings if notice is given to the publishers.

Printed and bound in China

THE SCIENCE OF
FORCES

PROJECTS AND EXPERIMENTS WITH FORCES AND MACHINES

STEVE PARKER

Heinemann Library
Chicago, Illinois

TABLETOP SCIENTIST

CONTENTS

From the force which keeps us on Earth, called gravity…

…to whirring motors and sparks caused by friction…

…to the complex and delicate gears in a clock, forces are at work around us all the time.

INTRODUCTION

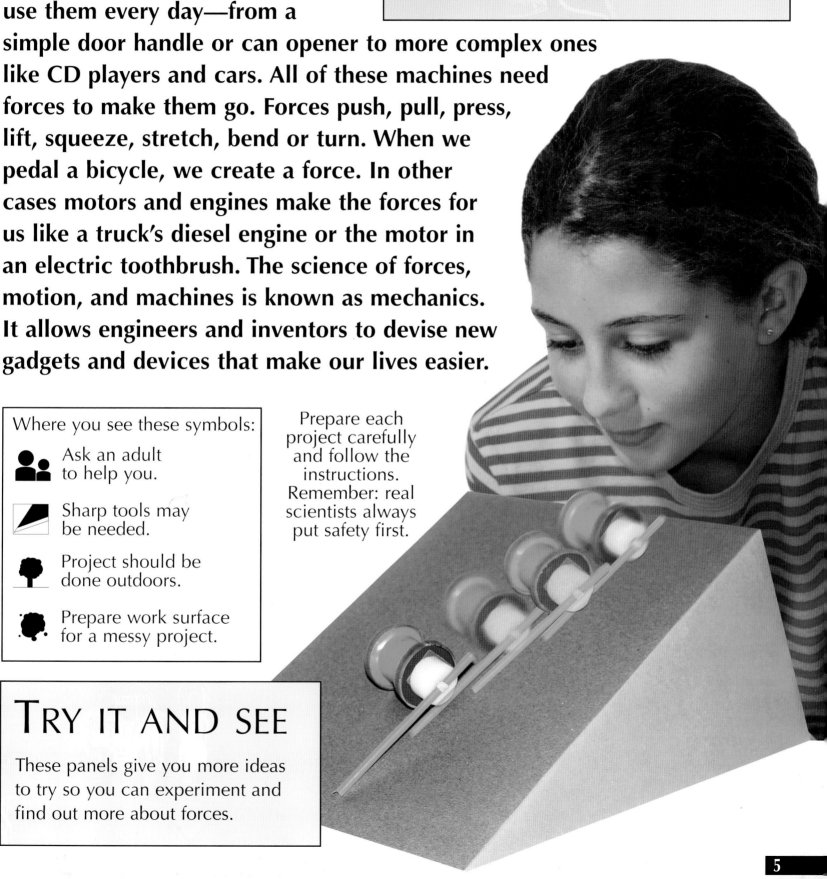

Machines, mechanical devices, and gadgets are everywhere. We use them every day—from a simple door handle or can opener to more complex ones like CD players and cars. All of these machines need forces to make them go. Forces push, pull, press, lift, squeeze, stretch, bend or turn. When we pedal a bicycle, we create a force. In other cases motors and engines make the forces for us like a truck's diesel engine or the motor in an electric toothbrush. The science of forces, motion, and machines is known as mechanics. It allows engineers and inventors to devise new gadgets and devices that make our lives easier.

HOW IT WORKS

These panels explain the scientific ideas in each project and the processes that make it work.

Where you see these symbols:

Ask an adult to help you.

Sharp tools may be needed.

Project should be done outdoors.

Prepare work surface for a messy project.

Prepare each project carefully and follow the instructions. Remember: real scientists always put safety first.

TRY IT AND SEE

These panels give you more ideas to try so you can experiment and find out more about forces.

FORCE ALL AROUND

One force acts on you and everything else all the time, everywhere you go—unless you're in deep space. This is the force of gravity. Any object has the pulling force of gravity. The amount of gravity depends on the object's mass. Earth is huge so its gravity is strong. It pulls objects down giving them what we call "weight."

Our planet's gravity extends 250,000 miles to the Moon and keeps it pulled near to Earth.

PROJECT: MAKE A WEIGHING MACHINE

WEIGHING MACHINE

WHAT YOU NEED

- **large and small cardboard boxes**
- **dowel**
- **cardboard**
- **thick marker pen**
- **thin and thick wire**
- **split-pin paper fastener**
- **plastic cup**
- **weights**
- **scissors**

1 PUSH THE DOWEL THROUGH THE LARGER BOX, FROM ONE SIDE TO THE OTHER, NEAR THE TOP.

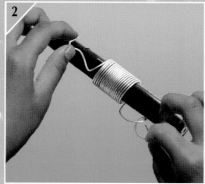

2 CURL THICK WIRE AROUND A MARKER PEN TO MAKE A SPRING. HANG IT ON THE DOWEL.

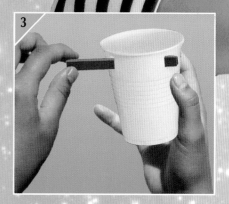

3 MAKE TWO SLITS IN A PLASTIC CUP. SLIDE A THIN PIECE OF CARDBOARD THROUGH FOR THE POINTER.

4 CUT A LONG SLOT IN ONE SIDE OF THE SMALLER BOX NEAR THE UPPER CORNER.

5 PUSH THE PAPER FASTENER THROUGH THE END OF THE POINTER AND INTO THE SLOT.

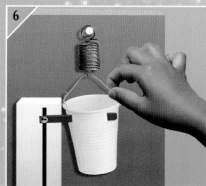

6 GLUE THE SMALLER BOX TO THE LARGER ONE. HANG THE CUP ON THE SPRING WITH THIN WIRE.

MASS & WEIGHT

All objects have mass. However, objects only have weight when the force of gravity acts on them. Earth's gravity pulls things that have mass toward the center of the planet. Gravity keeps us "stuck" to the surface of Earth! Far away in space there is no gravity and therefore no weight either.

SPRING STRETCHED

FORCE OF GRAVITY PULLS OBJECT DOWNWARD

MORE MASS = LONGER SPRING

ADJUST THE SPRING SO THE POINTER IS AT THE TOP OF THE SLOT WHEN THE CUP IS EMPTY. PUT AN ITEM SUCH AS A BALL BEARING OR PEBBLE INTO THE CUP. THE FORCE OF EARTH'S GRAVITY PULLS IT DOWN AND STRETCHES THE SPRING. THE POINTER SHOWS THE ITEM'S WEIGHT—THE AMOUNT OF GRAVITATIONAL PULL ON IT. ADD MORE ITEMS TO THE CUP. THEIR EXTRA MASS MEANS A GREATER PULL OF GRAVITY, MAKING THE SPRING LONGER.

EQUAL STRETCH

If you have many identical items, like toy building blocks or ball bearings, try adding them to the cup one at a time. Mark the position of the pointer each time with a pen. Are the spaces between the marks equal?

EQUALLY-SPACED MARKS MEAN THE SPRING STRETCHES BY THE SAME AMOUNT FOR THE SAME ADDED MASS. (THIS FOLLOWS A SCIENTIFIC RULE CALLED HOOKE'S LAW.) UNTIL THE LOAD BECOMES TOO HEAVY...

STOP AND GO FORCES

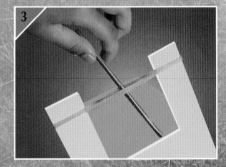

A soccerball does not move until you kick it. Any object that is not moving will stay still unless a force acts on it to make it go.

As a skydiver falls faster, air pushes back with increasing force until a steady speed is reached.

Once the object is moving it will keep going unless a force makes it slow down and stop. These forces are usually fairly obvious, such as brakes in a car.

In 1997 the force of Thrust SSC's jet engines was enough to make this car the world's speediest. It went faster than sound: 760 miles/h.

PROJECT: BUILD A CATAPULT

CATAPULT

WHAT YOU NEED

- **stiff cardboard**
- **straw**
- **elastic band**
- **small box**
- **test objects**
- **glue**
- **scissors**

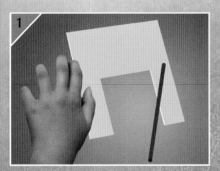

1 CUT A U-SHAPED FRAME OF STIFF CARDBOARD, THE SAME HEIGHT AS THE DRINKING STRAW.

2 CUT THE CORNER FROM A CARDBOARD BOX TO MAKE A TRIANGULAR BASE FOR THE U.

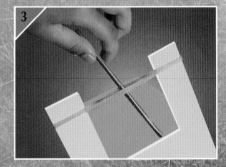

3 STRETCH AN ELASTIC BAND OVER THE U. PUT A STRAW THROUGH IT AND WIND IT AROUND.

4 POSITION THE STRAW SO ITS LOWER END RESTS ON THE FRONT OF THE FRAME'S BASE.

5 SLIT THE STRAW'S UPPER END. GLUE A ROUND PIECE OF CARDBOARD INTO IT FOR THE LAUNCH PAD.

FAST TO SLOW

The elastic band provides the firing force to launch the item. Why doesn't it keep going? Because of two other forces—gravity pulls the item down, and as the item pushes aside air, the air pushes back with a force called air resistance that slows it down.

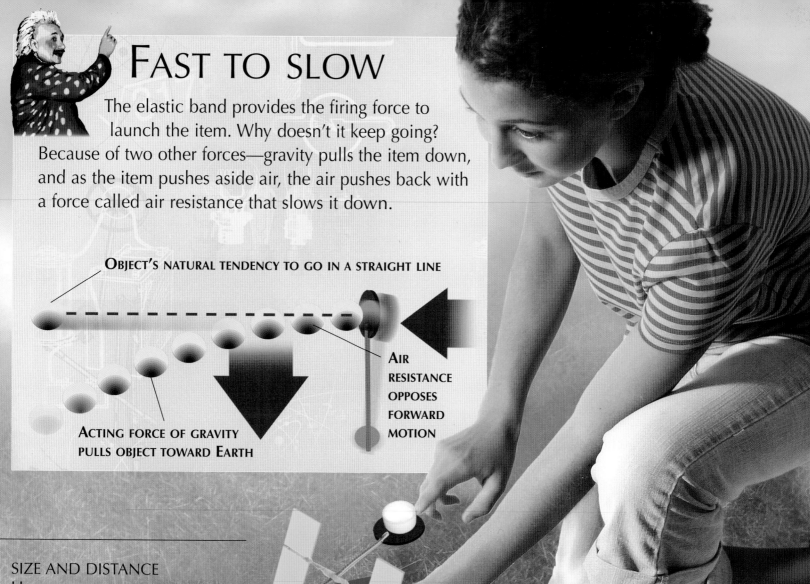

OBJECT'S NATURAL TENDENCY TO GO IN A STRAIGHT LINE

AIR RESISTANCE OPPOSES FORWARD MOTION

ACTING FORCE OF GRAVITY PULLS OBJECT TOWARD EARTH

SIZE AND DISTANCE
HOLD A SMALL ITEM LIKE AN ERASER ON THE LAUNCH PAD. PULL IT BACK SO THE STRAW IS HORIZONTAL, THEN FIRE! MEASURE HOW FAR IT GOES. TRY OBJECTS OF DIFFERENT SIZES AND WEIGHTS, LIKE A BALL OF TISSUE PAPER, A COIN OR A MARBLE.

MORE OR LESS

Try different amounts of firing force. For the same item, pull the launch pad back only a little way, then next time, as far as possible.

WEIGH DIFFERENT ITEMS AS SHOWN ON PAGE 7.
ARE HEAVIER ONES FIRED FARTHER?

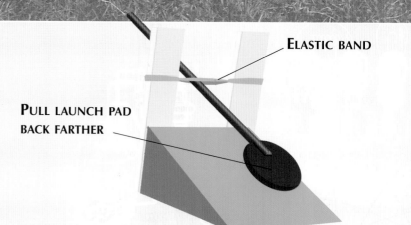

ELASTIC BAND

PULL LAUNCH PAD BACK FARTHER

GETTING GOING

Forces can make things move. If something is still, it needs a force to get it going. The more mass an object has, the more force is needed to do this. Also, the longer a force is applied, the faster the object moves.

A huge, heavy freight train has a large mass. It may take half an hour for the locomotive's tremendous pulling force to bring it up to a steady speed.

PROJECT: MAKE A FORCE METER

FORCE METER

WHAT YOU NEED

- **stiff cardboard**
- **thick foam board**
- **two beads**
- **elastic band**
- **strong thread**
- **eyelet**
- **push pin**
- **glue**
- **scissors**

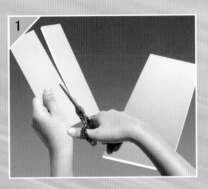

1. CUT A RECTANGLE OF STIFF CARDBOARD AND TWO SLIGHTLY SHORTER, MUCH NARROWER PIECES OF THICK FOAM BOARD.

2. TRIM A LONG EDGE OF EACH FOAM BOARD AT AN ANGLE, SO THEY FORM A V-SHAPED TUNNEL WHEN PUT TOGETHER.

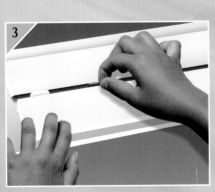

3. GLUE THE FOAM BOARD PIECES TO THE CARDBOARD, SO THE BEADS CAN SLIDE ALONG FREELY INSIDE THE TUNNEL FROM END TO END.

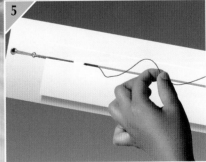

4. ATTACH AN ELASTIC BAND TO THE END OF THE CARDBOARD WITH A PUSH PIN. TIE IT TO THE THREAD. PASS THE THREAD THROUGH AN

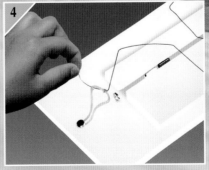

5. EYELET ATTACHED IN FRONT OF THE TUNNEL, KNOT IT, AND PASS IT THROUGH THE TWO BEADS.

FORCES MOVE MASS

Anything that moves has kinetic energy. If an object is still, a force must give it enough kinetic energy to move. Objects with a bigger mass have more kinetic energy when moving, so they need a larger force to get started. Vary the weight of the load in the truck and compare the readings on the force meter.

INCREASED LOAD

FORCE NEEDED TO MAKE TRUCK MOVE

HAUL AWAY!
GLUE ON A PAPER SCALE OF LINES. TIE A TOY WITH WHEELS SUCH AS A TRUCK TO THE STRING. GRADUALLY PULL IT HARDER WITH THE FORCE METER. NOTE THE SCALE READING JUST AS IT STARTS TO MOVE.

MORE MASS = MORE FORCE

Try loading a toy truck with identical weights, such as building blocks or ball bearings. As the load gets bigger in equal amounts, block by block, do the readings on the scale go up by equal amounts too?

SPEED UP, SLOW DOWN

A plane can cruise at the same speed for hours. But for takeoff it has to go faster and faster on the runway, and when landing, it has to lose speed. Large forces are needed to do this. Speeding up is acceleration. Slowing down is deceleration.

A dragster accelerates at 131 feet per second per second. After reaching a top speed of 310 miles/h, it needs a parachute to slow it down.

PROJECT: BUILD AN INK-DRIP ACCELEROMETER

INK-DRIP ACCELEROMETER

WHAT YOU NEED

- thick cardboard
- thread spools
- straws
- funnel
- pin
- ink
- modeling clay
- blotting paper
- tape
- scissors

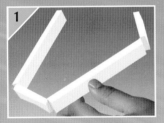

1 MAKE A CART FRAME OF THICK CARDBOARD TO FIT AROUND THE TWO THREAD SPOOLS.

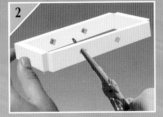

2 MAKE TWO HOLES IN THE SIDES OF THE CART FOR EACH STRAW AXLE.

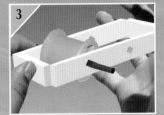

3 PUSH THE STRAWS THROUGH THE HOLES AND THREAD SPOOLS.

4 PUSH A SMALL BLOB OF MODELING CLAY INTO THE FUNNEL'S NARROW TIP. PIERCE WITH A PIN.

5 ADJUST THE PIERCED HOLE'S SIZE SO THAT INK IN THE FUNNEL EMERGES WITH REGULAR DRIPS.

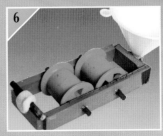

6 ATTACH THE EMPTY FUNNEL TO THE CART'S BACK. USE MODELING CLAY TO BALANCE IT.

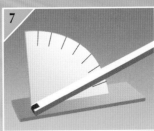

7 CUT A LONG RAMP OF CARDBOARD. TAPE TO THE CARDBOARD BASE. ADD A QUARTER-CIRCLE SCALE.

FASTER, FASTER

The force of gravity pulls the cart down the ramp. As the cart accelerates, gravity continues to pull, so the cart gains even more speed. The drips come out of the funnel at regular time intervals. If the ramp is at a steep angle, the cart accelerates more rapidly, and travels farther between each drip.

DRIP MARKS AT INCREASING INTERVALS SHOW ACCELERATION

EVEN GREATER SPACING MEANS HIGHER ACCELERATION

DRIP-DRIP FLYER
PUT A LONG STRIP OF BLOTTING PAPER ON THE RAMP FOR EACH RUN. ADD SOME INK TO THE FUNNEL, LIFT THE RAMP, AND LET THE CART GO. MAKE SURE THE CART AIMS STRAIGHT DOWN THE RAMP!

DOES MASS MATTER?

Changing the ramp's angle affects the rate of acceleration. What about changing the cart's mass? For the same angle, compare drips for the basic cart and with extra weight.

WEIGHT

White-hot gases forced downward from the rear of a rocket are its action. The reaction pushes the rocket upward—all the way into space.

ACT AND REACT

When you push a wall, you exert a force on it. Why doesn't the wall fall over? It pushes back with a force equal to your own but in the opposite direction. Your force is the action. The wall's is the reaction. This is part of a scientific law: "For every action there is an equal and opposite reaction."

Swimmers push the water powerfully backward. The reaction is their bodies are pushed forward.

PROJECT: BUILD AN ACTION/REACTION RAMP

ACTION/ REACTION RAMP

WHAT YOU NEED

- cardboard
- marbles
- string
- pencil
- glue
- scissors

1 MARK A SHALLOW CURVE ON CARDBOARD USING STRING WITH A PENCIL AT ONE END AND FIXED AT THE OTHER END.

2 CUT OUT THE SHAPE. PLACE IT ON CARDBOARD, TRACE AROUND IT AND CUT OUT A SECOND IDENTICAL SHAPE.

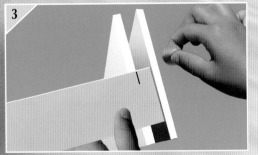

3 CUT SEVERAL NARROW STRIPS OF CARDBOARD, ALL THE SAME WIDTH— SLIGHTLY NARROWER THAN A MARBLE.

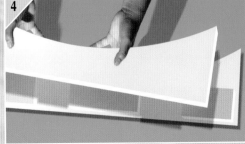

4 GLUE THE SHAPES TOGETHER WITH THE NARROW LENGTHS OF CARDBOARD IN-BETWEEN, FORMING A U-SHAPE.

PLACE EIGHT-TEN MARBLES IN THE BOTTOM OF THE RAMP. HOLD ANOTHER MARBLE AT ONE END, LET IT GO, AND CLICK! IT RUNS INTO THE ROW, KNOCKING THE MARBLE AT THE OPPOSITE END AWAY.

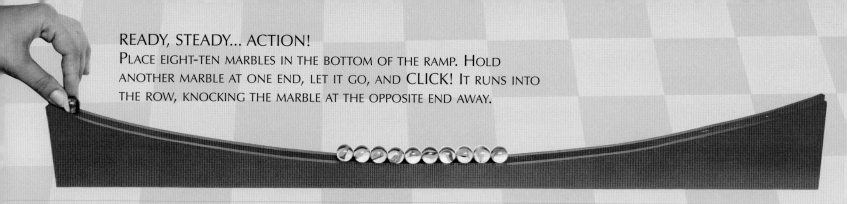

EQUAL HITS—ONE IN, ONE OUT

As the force of gravity pulls the marble down the slope, it gains more and more kinetic energy. When it hits the row of marbles, they push back with the same force in the opposite direction. The first marble stops, but its energy passes to the second marble, then third, and so on along the row. The last marble is free to move and rolls away. Then...

FIRST MARBLE HITTING ROW IS THE ACTION

REVERSE FORCE OF SECOND MARBLE IS THE REACTION

ENERGY OF FIRST MARBLE PASSES ALONG ROW TO LAST MARBLE, WHICH IS KNOCKED AWAY

ACTION

ACTION/REACTION ALONG ROW

FORCE OF GRAVITY OVERCOMES LAST MARBLE'S ENERGY AND PULLS IT BACK DOWN SLOPE AGAIN

ACTION/REACTION ALONG ROW

ENERGY TRANSFERRED IN OPPOSITE DIRECTION ALONG ROW, BACK TO FIRST MARBLE

ACTION

MORE MARBLES

Try increasing the force by releasing two marbles to roll down the ramp. Are two marbles knocked away from the other end? What about three, four, or more? Why do the back and forth movements gradually slow and stop? (Page 18 may give you one clue.)

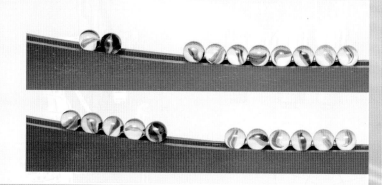

LOADS OF EFFORT

A lever can use a fairly small force at one end to produce a very large force at the other— enough to lift the lid off a paint can.

Can you lift a truck? Perhaps, if you had a lever long enough. A lever is a simple machine that alters a force. It is a stiff rod that tilts or pivots, from a place called the fulcrum. A lever can make a small force into a huge one. Levers range from the tiniest nail clippers to giant cranes.

The effort is the force needed to move a lever. A crane's tilting jib is like a lever with the fulcrum at one end, the effort near the other, and the load on the cable.

PROJECT: BUILD AN ADJUSTABLE LEVER

ADJUSTABLE LEVER

WHAT YOU NEED

- larger and smaller cardboard tubes
- cardboard sheet
- cardboard box
- string
- weights
- glue
- scissors

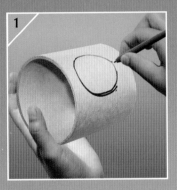

1 CUT A SHORT LENGTH FROM A WIDE CARDBOARD TUBE. TRACE AROUND A SMALLER TUBE ON EACH SIDE OF THE LARGER ONE.

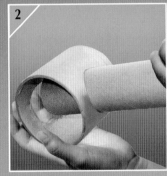

2 CUT AROUND THESE LINES TO MAKE TWO HOLES IN THE LARGER TUBE. PUSH THE SMALLER LEVER TUBE THROUGH THEM.

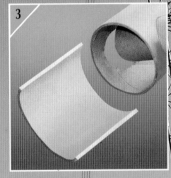

3 CUT A SLIGHTLY LONGER PIECE OF THE LARGER TUBE. THEN CUT THIS IN HALF TO MAKE A GUTTER-SHAPED CRADLE.

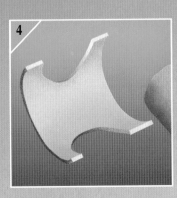

4 CUT A U SHAPED NOTCH IN EACH SIDE OF THE CRADLE, WIDE ENOUGH FOR THE SMALLER TUBE.

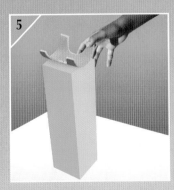

5 GLUE THE CRADLE TO THE TOP OF A TALL BOX. GLUE THIS TO A WIDE CARDBOARD BASE TO MAKE IT STABLE.

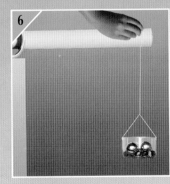

6 REST THE LEVER IN THE CRADLE OR FULCRUM. PREPARE LOOPED STRINGS FOR EFFORT AND LOAD.

FULCRUM CENTRAL

LIFT THE LOAD WITH YOUR OWN EFFORT. THEN TRY SLIDING THE TUBE SO THE FULCRUM IS NEARER ONE END.

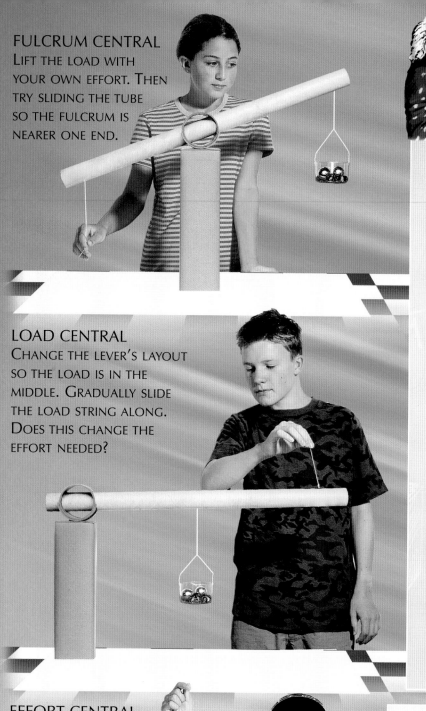

LOAD CENTRAL

CHANGE THE LEVER'S LAYOUT SO THE LOAD IS IN THE MIDDLE. GRADUALLY SLIDE THE LOAD STRING ALONG. DOES THIS CHANGE THE EFFORT NEEDED?

EFFORT CENTRAL

WITH THIS LAYOUT, TRY MOVING THE EFFORT NEARER THE FULCRUM, THEN NEARER THE LOAD.

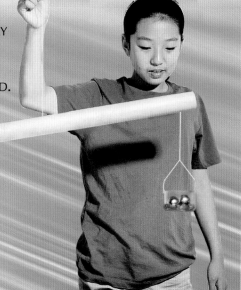

TRADE-OFF

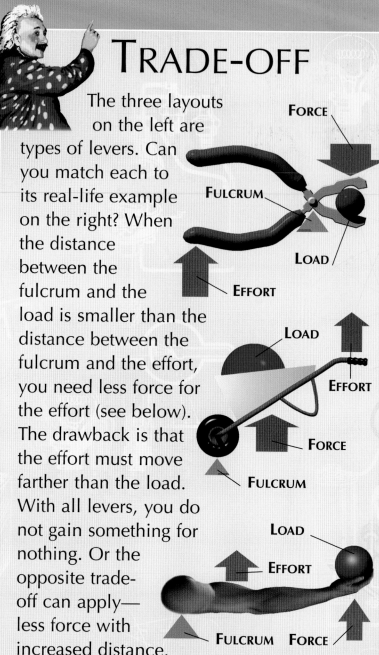

The three layouts on the left are types of levers. Can you match each to its real-life example on the right? When the distance between the fulcrum and the load is smaller than the distance between the fulcrum and the effort, you need less force for the effort (see below). The drawback is that the effort must move farther than the load. With all levers, you do not gain something for nothing. Or the opposite trade-off can apply— less force with increased distance.

FORCE

FULCRUM

LOAD

EFFORT

LOAD

EFFORT

FORCE

FULCRUM

LOAD

EFFORT

FULCRUM FORCE

BIGGER BUT SMALLER

As the position of the fulcrum changes, the force of the effort needed to move the same load also changes. Try measuring this changing effort with the weighing machine from page 7.

LONG DISTANCE TO EFFORT

SHORT DISTANCE TO EFFORT

Friction from a grinding disk is used to shape the hardest metal or rock.

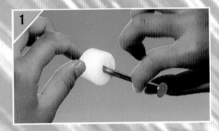

FORCE AND FRICTION

You need more force to drag a rough rock across stony ground, than to slide a smooth rock over slippery ice. As uneven surfaces rub and scrape against each other they oppose the force moving them. This is known as friction.

Ball bearings are made of very hard, smooth metal. They have almost no friction and therefore move smoothly.

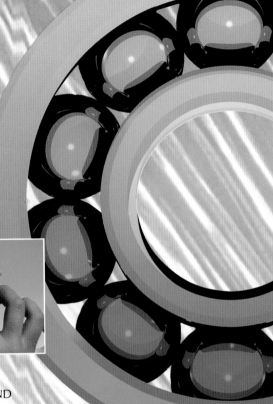

PROJECT: THE CLIMBING CRAWLER

CLIMBING CRAWLER

WHAT YOU NEED

- candle
- drinking straw
- elastic bands
- thread spool
- smooth plastic
- paper clip
- cardboard slope
- materials to put on slope
- nail

1
CUT A SHORT PIECE OF CANDLE. MAKE A HOLE THROUGH THE MIDDLE WITH A NAIL.

2
LOOP AN ELASTIC BAND OVER A SHORT STRAW AND THROUGH THE CANDLE'S HOLE.

3
PUT THE REST OF THE ELASTIC BAND THROUGH A THREAD SPOOL.

4
ATTACH THE BAND'S END TO THE REEL WITH A PAPER CLIP.

5
WIND UP THE ELASTIC BAND, USING THE STRAW AS A HANDLE.

5
TEST THE CRAWLER ON A SLOPE. NOTE HOW WELL IT CLIMBS.

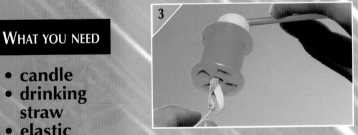

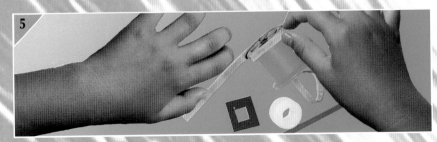

5
TRY SOME CHANGES. PUT SHORT ELASTIC BANDS AROUND THE REEL'S RIMS AND A PLASTIC "WASHER" BETWEEN THE CANDLE AND THE REEL.

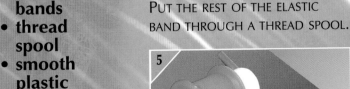

GRIP AND SLIP

Rough surfaces increase friction. Smooth ones reduce it. There is less friction acting on the straw's turning force where the candle rubs on the thread spool and more friction where the spool's rims rub on the slope.

WAX CANDLE SLIPS OVER PLASTIC WASHER

ELASTIC BAND RIM GRIPS PAPER SLOPE

FASTER CRAWLER
DOES THE "NEW IMPROVED" CRAWLER CLIMB THE SLOPE FASTER? DO ALL THE TESTS CAREFULLY, WINDING THE BAND THE SAME AMOUNT EACH TIME.

GRIPPIER, SLIPPIER

Try further improvements. Add a few drops of cooking oil lubricant between the candle and the plastic washer. Does this make the crawler climb better? Make the slope of rougher material, like sandpaper, then time the new crawler again.

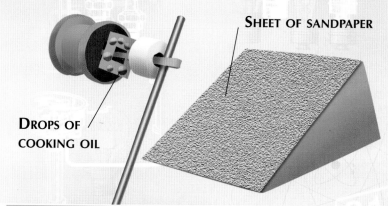

SHEET OF SANDPAPER

DROPS OF COOKING OIL

An ultra-fast spinning gyroscope has massive angular momentum, which makes it resist tilting.

AROUND AND AROUND

It takes a huge force to stop an oil tanker going at top speed. Moving objects tend to keep moving. This is momentum. The bigger an object and the faster it moves, the greater its momentum. This can be in a straight line or in a curve or circle, called angular momentum.

Without the inward pull of the chains, the people on a merry-go-round ride would fly off.

PROJECT: MAKE SOME SPINNING TOPS

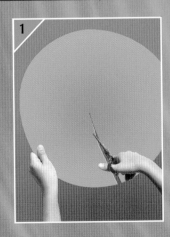

1

CUT OUT A DINNER-PLATE-SIZED CIRCLE OF STIFF CARDBOARD. MAKE A STRAIGHT SLIT FROM EDGE TO CENTER.

2

PULL THE EDGES OVER EACH OTHER AND TAPE THEM TO FORM A WIDE CONE ARENA. REST THIS IN A BASE, LIKE A BOWL.

3

CUT OUT SOME 4 INCH DISKS OF THICK CARDBOARD. DECORATE THEM WITH VARIOUS COLORS AND PATTERNS.

4

PUSH A SHORT, BLUNT PENCIL THROUGH EACH DISK'S CENTER, SO THAT ABOUT 1 INCH PENCIL LENGTH IS BENEATH.

FORCED TO SPIN

When you twirl the top, you apply a force to give it angular momentum. As the top turns, its shape means that a force, known as centripetal force, pulls the cardboard of the disk inward all the time. The tiny bits of cardboard making up the disk try to move in straight lines, according to the law of motion. But the strength of the cardboard prevents this from happening.

ANGULAR MOMENTUM

CENTRIPETAL FORCE

CARDBOARD'S STRENGTH KEEPS DISK INTACT

MORE = MORE?

A top's momentum depends on its mass and its speed. Make a top heavier with modeling clay. It needs a bigger force to start but does it spin for longer?

TRY ADDING THE CLAY AS A LUMP AROUND THE CENTER OR AS A RING AROUND THE DISK'S RIM.

MODELING CLAY

TWIRLING TOPS AT TOP SPEED
PUT A TOP IN THE CONE ARENA, HOLDING IT BY THE UPPER END OF THE PENCIL. FLICK YOUR FINGERS TO MAKE IT TWIRL AROUND. PRACTICE THIS MOVEMENT SO THE TOP INCREASES SPINNING SPEED OVER A SECOND OR SO, RATHER THAN TRYING TO TWIRL IT FAST IMMEDIATELY. THE TOP TURNS... AND TURNS... STAYING UPRIGHT FOR SOME TIME. AS IT SLOWS, IT STARTS TO WOBBLE. FINALLY IT TIPS ONTO ITS EDGE AND STOPS. HOW LONG CAN YOU KEEP A TOP SPINNING?

PULLING POWER

A pulley is a wheel with raised rims, so that a rope, cable, or chain fits around it. One pulley can change the direction of a force, so that if you pull a rope downward, the load moves upward. Two pulleys make it easier to raise the load.

Sets of pulleys are common on cranes, hoists, elevators, and sailing ships. They allow a small pulling force to move a large load—even a huge, heavy sail filled with wind.

PROJECT: BUILD A TWO-PULLEY HOIST

TWO-PULLEY HOIST

WHAT YOU NEED

- thick cardboard
- cardboard tube or dowel
- foam board
- string
- glue
- scissors

CUT OUT FOUR LARGE CIRCLES, ALL OF THE SAME SIZE, FROM THICK CARDBOARD.

CUT TWO SLIGHTLY SMALLER CIRCLES FROM THICK FOAM BOARD.

SANDWICH EACH SMALLER CIRCLE BETWEEN TWO LARGER ONES. GLUE TO MAKE A PULLEY.

CUT SIDES FOR THE UPPER FRAME FROM THICK CARD AS SHOWN, USING ONE PULLEY AS A GUIDE.

CUT THE LOWER FRAME SIDES IN A SIMILAR WAY USING THE OTHER PULLEY AS THE GUIDE.

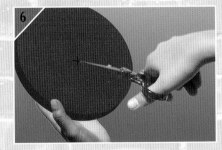

CUT AN X-SHAPED DOUBLE-SLOT IN THE CENTER OF EACH OF THE PULLEY WHEELS.

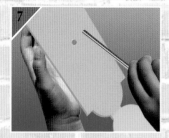

7 USING A STRAW AS A GUIDE CUT A ROUND HOLE IN THE CENTER OF EACH HOUSING FLAP.

8 FILL TWO SHORT LENGTHS OF STRAW WITH MODELING CLAY AND PUSH ONE EACH THROUGH THE TOP AND BOTTOM HOUSINGS AND PULLEY WHEELS.

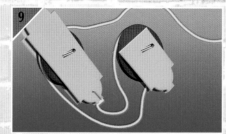

9 ATTACH THE HOUSINGS. TIE ROPE TO A HOLE IN THE BOTTOM OF THE TOP HOUSING. RUN IT THROUGH THE LOWER PULLEY AND BACK THROUGH THE TOP PULLEY.

MORE FOR LESS?

Pulleys work like levers (see page 16). Winding the rope around two pulleys means that a load can be lifted by only half the pulling force, used with one pulley. But, like a lever, you do not gain this extra pulling power for nothing. The load only moves half as far with two pulleys, compared to one. So you pull with half the force but for twice as long.

UPPER PULLEY

PULLEY FRAME

ROPE WINDS AROUND BOTH PULLEYS

LOWER PULLEY

LOAD

FORCE OF GRAVITY

PULLING FORCE

MAKE A HOLE AND TIE THE TOP PULLEY TO A BEAM.

HEAVE! HAUL UP A LOAD WITH BOTH PULLEYS. THEN CHANGE THE ROPE TO USE THE TOP PULLEY ONLY. DO YOU NEED LESS OR MORE PULLING FORCE?

ADD MORE PULLEYS

Each time a pulley is added to the hoist, the pulling force needed gets smaller. But the amount of rope becomes longer and longer, and friction increases too. Try your hoist with three pulleys.

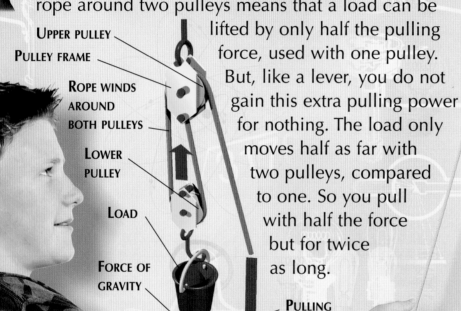

TOP PULLEY

INTERMEDIATE PULLEY

BOTTOM PULLEY

TIE A BUCKET TO THE BOTTOM PULLEY WITH ROPE.

23

Around Along

One of the simplest machines is the screw. It's a slope or ramp wound around a central pole. Like the lever and pulley, the screw alters forces. It can change a small turning or rotating force into a much more powerful force that pulls, splits, lifts, or tightens.

A staircase is a simple slope. A "spiral" staircase is a slope twisted around a central pole. One big advantage of a "spiral" staircase is that it takes up less space than a normal one.

Project: Make a screw lift

Screw lift

What you need

- large and small cardboard tubes
- clear plastic or cellophane
- cardboard
- glue
- tape
- scissors
- ruler
- compass
- small foam packing peanuts

1 Cut a length of large tube and a slightly longer length of small tube. Measure from the center to the edge of both.

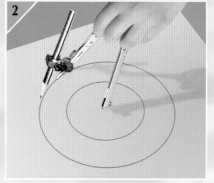

2 Use the measurements to draw two circles on clear plastic, one inside the other. Draw a circle 1/2-inch wider.

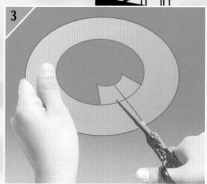

3 Mark two flaps side by side, inside the circles. Cut along the lines to make a spiral strip. Make 5 or 6 of these.

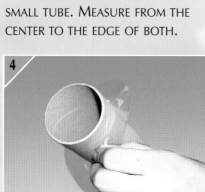

4 Make a slit at a slight angle at one end of the narrower tube. Push in one flap. Curl the plastic around the tube.

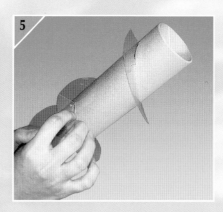

5 Pull the strip to make part of a screw shape. Mark the position of the other flap, cut a slot and insert it.

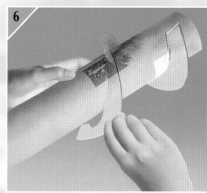

6 Insert one flap of a second strip into the slot made in step 5. Repeat steps 4 and 5 for this second strip.

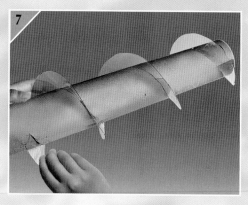

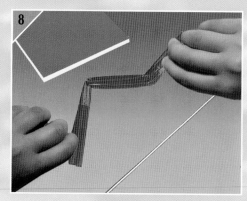

REPEAT STEPS 4, 5, AND 6 WITH THE OTHER STRIPS SO THEY OVERLAP AS A SCREW SHAPE THAT WINDS NEATLY ALONG THE TUBE. TEST THIS SCREW IN THE LARGER TUBE SLEEVE. IF IT IS TOO TIGHT, ADJUST THE STRIPS BY MAKING THEIR SLOTS FARTHER APART SO EACH STRIP ANGLES FLATTER AGAINST THE TUBE. IF THE SCREW IS TOO LOOSE, MAKE THE SLOTS CLOSER.

MAKE A HANDLE FROM THREE STRAWS TAPED OR TIED TOGETHER AND BENT IN AN L-SHAPE. GLUE OR TAPE ONE END OF THE L TO A SQUARE OF STIFF CARDBOARD. YOU CAN STRENGTHEN THIS HANDLE WITH BENT WIRE IF NECESSARY.

INSERT THE SQUARE CARDBOARD OF THE HANDLE INTO SLOTS IN ONE END OF THE SCREW. PUT THE SCREW INTO ITS SLEEVE.

TURN TO LIFT
TRY LIFTING SMALL, LIGHT ITEMS LIKE FOAM PACKING PEANUTS. PUT THE LOWER END OF THE SCREW-AND-SLEEVE INTO A BOWL OF THEM, TURN—AND UP THEY COME! CUT A "WINDOW" IN THE SLEEVE TUBE TO SEE HOW IT WORKS.

TURN OF THE SCREW

The Archimedes' screw uses the same principle as a metal household screw. While the screw stays in position the turning force pulls the material (foam peanuts) upward. The Archimedes' screw was invented to lift water from one level to another.

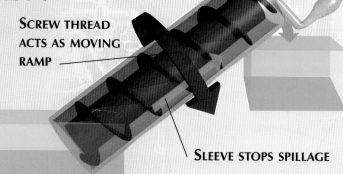

SCREW THREAD ACTS AS MOVING RAMP

SLEEVE STOPS SPILLAGE

GET IN GEAR

Gears can change a force in various ways. Depending on how many cogs or teeth they have, they can increase or decrease the turning speed of a force and make it more powerful. Many cogs can be used in different combinations.

Clocks use many cogs to make the hands turn very slowly. The little hand turns just once in twelve hours!

Bicycle gears let the rider pedal at the same speed with the same force, whether going uphill or going down.

PROJECT: EXPERIMENT WITH COGS

COGS

WHAT YOU NEED

- **cardboard**
- **straws**
- **corrugated cardboard**
- **cardboard box**
- **string**
- **glue**
- **scissors**
- **modeling clay**

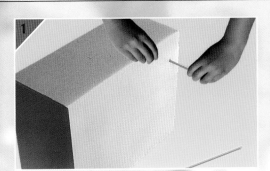

MAKE TWO OPPOSITE HOLES NEAR ONE END OF A TALL, NARROW BOX. FEED A STRAW THROUGH THE HOLES.

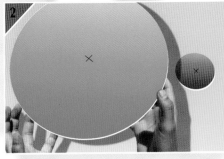

CUT OUT A LARGE AND A SMALL DISK FROM STIFF CARDBOARD. IN THE CENTER OF EACH MAKE TWO SLITS IN AN X-SHAPE.

CUT STRIPS OF CORRUGATED CARDBOARD. GLUE THEM AROUND THE EDGE OF THE DISKS TO MAKE GEAR TEETH.

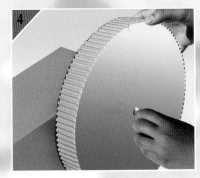

PUSH THE LARGER GEARWHEEL FIRMLY ONTO THE STRAW. PUT A LUMP OF MODELING CLAY ON THE END OF THE STRAW.

HOLD THE LITTLE DISK SO ITS TEETH MESH WITH THE BIG ONE, MARK ITS CENTER POINT. ATTACH IT AS IN STEP 4. PUT ARROWS ON THE GEARS.

TURNS AND TEETH

ROTATE THE SMALLER GEAR. HOW MANY TIMES DOES IT TURN FOR ONE TURN OF THE LARGER GEAR? IS THIS SIMILAR TO THE COMPARISON OF THE NUMBER OF TEETH ON THE GEARS? TRY TURNING THE LARGER GEAR. DO YOU HAVE TO USE MORE TURNING FORCE?

UP OR DOWN

Two same-sized gears change a clockwise turning force into an counterclockwise one. If a large gearwheel drives a small one, turning speed rises but turning force falls. This is "gearing up." The opposite is "gearing down." The number of teeth on one gear, compared with the number on the other, is the gear ratio. If the ratio is 2:1, the turning speed goes up two times but the turning force halves.

TRANSFER GEARS

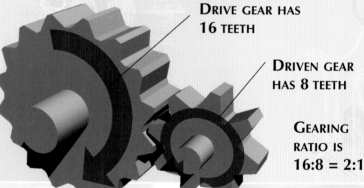

DRIVE GEAR HAS 16 TEETH

DRIVEN GEAR HAS 8 TEETH

GEARING RATIO IS 16:8 = 2:1

MORE GEARS

Add more gearwheels to make a gear train. Some machines use gear trains to make different parts turn at their own speeds but keep moving at the same time.

INTERMEDIATE GEARS

A car's gear shift lever works about a dozen main gearwheels in the gearbox. They mesh in different combinations for first gear, second, third, and so on.

GEARS GALORE

Gears not only change turning speed and force. They can also alter turning direction—at right angles, clockwise to counterclockwise, and so on. There are several types of gears, each designed to transfer a certain amount of force in a particular way, and also to turn or run at a certain speed.

PROJECT: MAKE SOME TRANSFER GEARS

WHAT YOU NEED

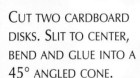

- cardboard box
- cardboard tube
- cardboard
- thick string
- glue
- large nails
- scissors
- long, thin cardboard box
- straws
- pencil
- ruler
- compass

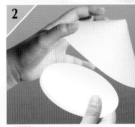

1 CUT TWO CARDBOARD DISKS. SLIT TO CENTER, BEND AND GLUE INTO A 45° ANGLED CONE.

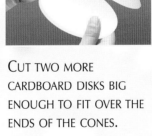

2 CUT TWO MORE CARDBOARD DISKS BIG ENOUGH TO FIT OVER THE ENDS OF THE CONES.

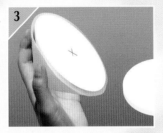

3 MAKE X-SHAPED SLITS IN THE CENTER OF EACH DISK. GLUE THE DISKS ONTO THE CONES.

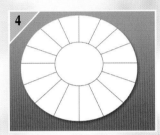

4 DRAW A CIRCLE ON CARDBOARD. DIVIDE IT INTO 16 EQUAL SEGMENTS AND CUT THESE OUT.

5 GLUE 8 SEGMENTS TO EACH CONE WITH SPACES IN BETWEEN.

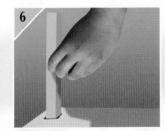

6 GLUE A STRIP OF THICK CARDBOARD NEAR THE EDGE OF THE BOX.

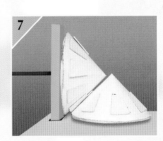

7 PUT THE CONES ON STRAW AXLES AND POSITION AS SHOWN.

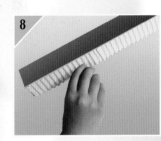

8 STICK A CORRUGATED CARDBOARD STRIP TO A LONG, THIN BOX "RACK."

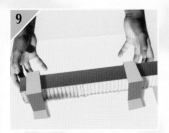

9 CUT CARDBOARD BRACKETS TO HOLD THE RACK ON THE BASE AND LET IT SLIDE.

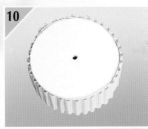

10 MAKE A GEARWHEEL (SEE PAGE 26) WITH A NAIL AXLE.

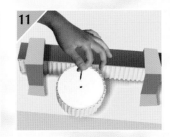

11 ATTACH THE GEARWHEEL'S AXLE TO THE BASE SO IT MESHES WITH THE RACK.

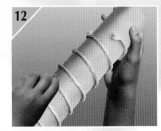

12 WIND THICK STRING AROUND A TUBE AND GLUE IN PLACE.

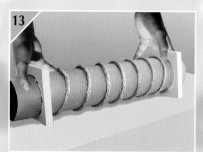

13

14

MAKE BRACKETS OF THICK CARDBOARD, WITH HOLES FOR THE TUBE. ATTACH THEM TO THE BASE SO THE TUBE TURNS BUT CANNOT SLIDE OUT.

MAKE ANOTHER GEARWHEEL AND ATTACH IT TO THE BASE WITH A STRAW AXLE TO MESH WITH THE TUBE.

WORM AND PINION
THE WORM'S TURNING MOTION MAKES THE PINION (GEARWHEEL) TURN SLOWLY.

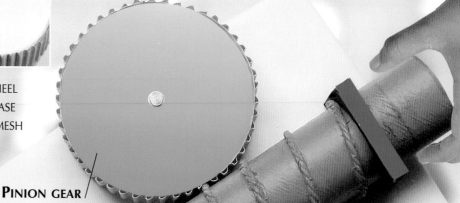

PINION GEAR

WORM GEAR

PINION GEAR

RACK

RACK AND PINION
A TURNING FORCE AT THE PINION IS CHANGED INTO A SLIDING OR BACK-AND-FORTH FORCE AT THE RACK. OR THE OPPOSITE CAN HAPPEN.

BEVEL GEARS
WHEN ONE BEVEL GEAR IS TURNED, THE OTHER ONE ROTATES AT THE SAME SPEED. THE WAY THAT THE BEVEL GEARS FIT TOGETHER MEANS THAT THE DIRECTION OF THE FORCE CAN BE CHANGED BY 90°.

BEVEL GEARS

NEW DIRECTIONS

The turning force of one bevel gearwheel transfers through a right angle, 90°, to the second bevel. The turning force of the worm transfers to the pinion, through 90°. The force is now parallel to the axle of the worm. Unlike the bevel gears or the rack and pinion, the worm does not work in reverse: moving the pinion does not move the worm.

BEVEL GEARS

WORM AND PINION

RACK AND PINION

HISTORY OF FORCES

360 B.C.E. In ancient Greece, famous scientist and thinker Aristotle discovered that falling objects gain speed, or accelerate, as they fall. He believed that a heavier object falls faster than a lighter one of the same size and shape.

1581–83 During church services, Galileo Galilei noticed how bell ropes and hanging lamps swing in the breezes. He timed the movements using his own pulse (heartbeat). He found the time for each swing was the same whether the rope swings a long way or a little. He also discovered that all objects with the same size and shape gain speed at the same rate when dropped, no matter what weight they are.

1590 Galileo's *De Motu (On Motion)* described his experiments with falling objects. Around this time, it's said he dropped objects such as cannonballs from the Leaning Tower of Pisa in Italy. He wanted to prove his new ideas about force and motion.

1638 Galileo published one of the greatest science books, *Discourses Concerning Two New Sciences.*

1665–66 Isaac Newton described his three laws of motion. One of the laws states that force is needed to change the speed or direction of moving objects. Another one says that every force (action) has an equal and opposite reaction. He also had ideas about gravity as a universal force that acted everywhere.

1676 Robert Hooke described how the stretch of a spring is related to the force pulling it (Hooke's Law).

1684 Newton published his landmark book, *The Mathematical Principles of Natural Philosophy,* known as the *Principia.*

1905 Albert Einstein described his theory of special relativity, involving forces and motions at high speeds.

1915 Einstein wrote a scientific report about his theory of general relativity. This replaced Newton's ideas for calculating forces and motions at very fast speeds.

1960 The International General Conference on Weights and Measures defined the unit of force as the newton. One newton accelerates a mass of one kilogram at a rate of one meter per second per second.

Glossary

Accelerate to go faster, gaining more speed for each unit of time. If speed is measured in feet per second, then acceleration is measured in feet per second per second.

Air resistance force that slows an object passing through air as the object tries to push aside the tiny particles which make up air. It is a form of friction.

Decelerate to go slower, losing more speed for each unit of time

Force push, pull, squeeze, bend, stretch, or similar action that tries to change the movement of an object in some way—its speed, or direction, or both

Fulcrum pivot of a lever, the point at which it tilts or swings

Friction force that opposes movement when objects rub and scrape past each other. The movement is changed into heat and other forms of energy.

Gear ratio usually, a comparison of the number of teeth or cogs on one gearwheel, compared to the number on the other gearwheel

Gravity pulling force or attraction that occurs between all objects that have mass, from a single tiny atom to a massive galaxy in space

Kinetic energy energy of movement or motion, that depends on the mass of an object and how fast it travels (see also Momentum)

Mass amount of matter in an object

Momentum tendency of an object to keep moving in the same direction at the same speed

Weight force an object feels due to gravity. Weight depends on the amount of mass an object has and how strong gravity is. The moon has less gravity than earth and so we would weigh less there than we do here.

INDEX